# Marsden Bay
## James Kirkup

Red Squirrel Press

First Published in the UK in 2008
by Red Squirrel Press
PO Box 219 Morpeth  NE61 9AU
www.redsquirrelpress.com


Cover Image:
Marsden Bay (1898) by George Blackie Sticks
© Tyne & Wear Museums

To Makoto Tamaki

ISBN 978-1-906700-03-4

Printed in the UK by Athenaeum Press Ltd
Gateshead, Tyne & Wear

.

I dedicate this book to my great friend Dorothy Fleet
(Dearest of Dorothies)

# Contents

## The Meaning

A light wind went down
with the declining sun,
and a great stillness filled
the late autumn afternoon.

The bamboos hung motionless,
the crows fell silent in the cryptomerias,
the waters in the lake stopped rippling
and even a passing cloud was stilled.

Only for a moment. Then
everything began to move and sound again.
 – What was the reason for – no,
the meaning of that sudden stop?

And why did I, too, stop?

## A Tomb in China

The dank waters of an ancient canal
feed an even more ancient pond, both
dull white under a sky of slate.

Not a soul to be seen here – melancholy
solitude, rare in this overcrowded province.

"Most people don't like to come here..."

The mausoleum of an unknown empress
rises on the other bank,
hardly visible in a vast cedar grove
walled-in on all sides.

Weatherworn marble porticos
lead to an avenue of votive monuments
their moss and lichens the only colours
in the monotone day: their pallid shapes
melt away into the shadowy glades
of centenarian cedars –
all far off, almost remote abodes
reflected on the tin mirror of the pond
as long, moveless spectres of neglect,
the very images of forgotten life, forgotten death.

Giant lotuses, transfixed by the cold,
bend long stalks over the leaden lake
where only slowly-widening rings
mark the drippings of gathered dews
running mercurial from rusted leaves.

Among the reeds, a few skulls floating.

## Five Tanka

Our love was something
never expected to last –
at least on my part.
But here we are, years later,
our garden still in flower.

Simple things are best,
you say, and I agree. But
is love as simple
as we think? What mystery
preserves it for us?

When I first saw you,
did you notice me at all?
I think so, despite
pretended indifference –
I make you pay for that now!

Sometimes I wake, and
watch you sleeping – a marvel
that you can love me
even in a dream, and not
forget our waking kisses.

You murmured my name
in sleep, and I heard it in
a dream of passion
that made me turn again to
love that lives beyond the dream.

## Mirage

The mountains of Mongolia appear
to float on air and cloud – shapes
cut from rose and violet papers.

Through veils of gauze
the mirage that is Beijing –
monumental roofs and waterfalling stairways
all carved and gilded,
weightless white marble in a dream
of dust before the frontier of the steppes
hanging in leagues of early winter light
that brings them closer
then casts them far away, and further –
beyond their real or imagined world
in space and time and memory.
.

## Intrusions

Now I keep dreaming someone else's dreams.
These cities, faces, houses, gardens I have never known
seem sometimes almost cruelly familiar, and yet
impenetrably foreign, alien, neither here nor there.

I think I know these streets, but forget their names.
I see these figures, faces, but only half recognize
their smiling or indignant owners. I pay attention to
their language, understanding without knowing it.

Is it someone else's memories of other times
I inhabit in my absent, labouring overtimes of sleep?
Why does he keep showing me these things? Why
does he try to make me feel at home here

in a world where I am lost, abandoned, lonely and
utterly confused, a helpless foreigner
wandered from another planet, another way
of waking life that once I shared with him

and cannot quite recollect now, or reconstruct.
– So I go wandering from street to square,
looking for nonexistent buses, departed trains,
entering houses that must once have been my own

but now are hostels for the blind, the dispossessed
and where my modest privacy is casually invaded by
the lives of people I have never met before, who
regard me sidelong, as they would a mad intruder.

Even more peculiar, the apparitions of all those
I once knew – parents, friends, enemies, lovers,
the dead, the undead, the dying, the victims of revenge
who suddenly confront me out of nowhere (now a real place)

with outraged gesturings, contorted visages racked
by suffering, mockery, fear or madness. They spit at me,
but I can have no pity on them now, however much they plead –
they come from someone else's dreams, and I am dead to them.

## The Midnight Carol Singers

Where are they now?
Through what centuries of dreams
they come to me, the memories
of voices singing in the dark,
singing to a waking child –
now near, now infinitely far,
like angels' voices in the back lane,
on the quayside, along the bay?

What unknown carol singers in the snows
of midnight, in the frosts of time?
Singing of birth that is death,
of peace that is war,
of love that is hatred,
of the divine that is lost?

And where is that dark-haired midnight visitor,
come on the stroke of twelve to bring
a good new year, his trouser pockets
filled with lumps of coal, offering them
for luck, in hands black with fate?

Where are they all now?
Only these innocent memories survive.

## Sonnet

Streets turn cold in the wind. Asylum walls
pale perplexedly with the northern sky
falling with snow-light through the arctic halls
of faded stations that the trains pass by.

The complicated hosts along the quays
build black scaffoldings against the bare white
of clouds converging in celestial seas
that freeze out star-frost on the wicked night.

Leaving uneasy streets of curving steel
I turn into the warm and wooden lane
where lamps pick out the ruts of hoarded rain.

Whatever I have felt, I shall not feel,
nor find again what I had lately found.

The leaves are done, and fallen to the ground.

## Privileged Being

His life one long underpass
beneath a railway bridge, a highway.
Or on the post-office steps, outside
the cathedral after mass, he waits
patiently. Or in a darkened shop doorway,
eyes lowered, hands at his sides,
wearing the same old garments,
once of good quality, now tattered,
he stands silently, ghost with gleaming eyes.

He listens to snatches of foolish talk,
collecting memories of squandered words
and the laughter of certain passers-by.
When it's fine, he sits in a quiet corner
of a park, away from the playground,
the tennis court, the bowling green.
There he gathers bird song, the wind
in the trees, the scent of flowerbeds.

He drinks at the fountain like a sparrow,
gives the ruffled beard a splash,
picks half a sandwich from the rubbish bin,
fits his lips to someone else's bite,
the only kind of kiss he knows.

His life is dangerous solitude, invaded
by cruel children, drunken hooligans.
He has no companions. A crowd increases
misery enough for one. And is content with
his own thoughts, his own entertainment.

Now and then, someone gives him a few coins.
He accepts them. He does not say thank you.
There is no thankfulness in constant fear.
All he knows is, it is already
privilege enough to be still alive.

## Summer of 1939

The last class of the afternoon.
Summer. Outside, the chestnuts heavy with leaf,
the ships hooting for pilots from the harbour,
the water-cart sprinkling streets of dusty sand.

In the classroom, the smell of boys' bodies,
the rustle of paper in this 'silent reading' period.
His favourite class, but boredom for the others,
the footballers, rugger lads and cricketers
slouched over *Nicholas Nickleby* or *Silas Marner*
while he was totally rapt by *Stalkey and Co.*

Friday. The weekend feeling of cricket, the baths.
But the rustling paper is not just the pages of books
being slowly turned. Under the teacher's nose, a note
is being circulated, with the urgent instruction:
"Pass it on" in a stage whisper. – A nudging elbow,
and the message falls across his open book:
"After school, in the bike shed, Ted Gray is going to
slaughter that swot –" "– that swot? Who?"
His own name swims before him, misspelt as usual.
Why Ted Gray? He hardly knows him, never spoke to him.

But some conspiracy unknown to him
has urged Ted Gray on to fight – for no reason.
He feels his face grow pale – paler than usual,
then red with embarrassment, with sick fear.

"Pass it on!" someone hisses.
He passes it on, but the teacher notices.
"Bring me that paper, boy!" He reads it.
He knows he can save me from the slaughter.
But all he does is crumple the note and say:

"Good luck!" He grins. Waves of laughter from the class.
Only a few minutes to the end of the lesson.
I look nervously at Ted Gray, one of the school bullies.
He, too, is grinning at me, showing his big fists.

– It all fizzled out. When the bell rang,
everybody made a rush for home, for the beach.
I ran like the wind through quiet back lanes
till I reached the cool refuge
of the Public Library and Reading Room in Ocean Road,
the glassy shades of the Local History Collection.
There my racing heart slowly calmed down.

But there was a war brewing. I was sixteen.
Millions of people, without knowing it
going to their deaths in the summer sunshine.
Summer of 1939.

## Sarcophagus

Invading the sacred pyramid
a shrine defended only by
my spirit's undying power
was easy. The spirit has other means.

So unwind them gently,
these cerements they bound me in
swaddling me like a new-born child
in secret layers of spice, balm, fard.

Within the outer carapace
you found the invisible man
of your H.G. Wells movie –
Claude Rains, a disembodied voice.

That carapace was empty cloth,
shallow and too neatly-folded
with surgical precision. Mine
is an extension of my earthly self

an endless roll of grave garments
symbolizing everlasting life –
if you cut it, you cut my fate,
so use no scissors to unravel me.

Then only may you analyze
the unguents, herbs and balsams
of the embalmer's divine craft.
It was he who encapsulated me

beyond the dust and sand and ashes
of my native kingdom, to be a pharaoh
forever, beyond the science that
registers my fingerprints, my teeth, my hair.

For you lay bare not only man
in all his puny bifurcation,
but a land, a civilization preserved
for him alone, and not for you, intruder.

– So handle me with care, if you would know
my secrets, and the message of the past
that is beyond all measurement, and almost
beyond belief, beyond imagination.

## For a Friend who Died of AIDS

The last days were terrible
because he was suffering
he was suffering so abominably.

He fell sick at a time
when there was an intermission
in the treatment of the disease.

When life could be prolonged
but suffering could not be relieved:
the root of the ill could not be reached.

We stayed with him
at the hospital and were there
when he died.

He died in the course of
a chemotherapy perfusion –
his last chance.

The doctor to whom he was so attached
was holding his hand.
I had my arm round his shoulders.

The last days were so terrible
because he was suffering
he was suffering abominably.

We stayed with him
at the hospital and we were there
when he died.

## Parting and Meeting

You went away again
though you did not want to leave.
I let you go away.

We miss each other –
as soon as we are apart
we miss each other.

We cannot live without
one another, yet we are always
parting, for parting is the beginning

of meeting, and meeting
the beginning of parting.
– So I wait here for your return

alone but happy because I know
you will come back again and
I will come back to you.

We never speak of it.
We never mention the word.
But is this what they call love?

## Two Calligraphies

Rain illuminates
ancient stones, incscribes
new messages along their flanks
and on their sunbaked intransigence
bearing the weathers of lost seasons
and the coming winter
in first calligraphies of snow.

*

The sunset cloud, a shadowy tree
spreads its leaning trunk
its branches, twigs, fans of leaves across
the darkening screen of the entire sky,
commanding a sense of balance in the composition
worthy of an unknown oriental master
who almost imperceptibly lets it change
then rapidly dissolve into a shapeless
maze that alters time and space
in estuaries with innumerable mouths
greeting the ark of the new moon.

## Lines to be Inscribed on a Japanese Kite

Finder, wherever I fall, that place
is the one I hoped for; whether it be
on factory or temple roof or field of rice,
on Matsushima's islands or the Inland Sea,
on snowy mountain flank or in the lee
of a fisherman's boat, within the riven
shadow of his leaning sail – I see
your finder's hand draw up my kite to heaven
as if, from the endlessness of space
you chose before all others my peculiar face
and translated from a quiet star
into your own wild tongue
these words with which I launch the air
and that the wind carries without care
to you, finder, like a falling song.

## The Dr Jekyll and Mr Hyde Syndrome
## or
## Phineas Gage no longer Phineas Gage

An iron bar transpierces
a human head from cheek
to crown, eliminating
the left eye and part
of the frontal lobe.
Intellectual faculties
still intact, Gage
is no longer the Gage we knew.

A cancellation of
personality, a mind
honest and trustworthy
transformed into the brain
of a raving monster –
and all because of the accidental destruction of
the ventro-median cortex.

# Unease

From time to time there come
those days when nothing seems to happen,
when evenings are long and still
and nights all starry wakefulness.

The very peacefulness brings unease,
disquiet indefinable, almost as if
awaiting the catastrophe that never comes,
until its looming presence stirs a breeze.

Somewhere far off, but not too far away
wars light horizons with other sunsets,
the dead dying in bitter rains
are comforted by darker dawns.

Between times, between seasons
one lingering ghostly in the other
waiting for release, for the fulfilment of
a certain resolution, or an uncertain fate.

## The Day Ahead

Born of black night –
the first breath of pink
on dawn clouds is always
perfect, never vulgar,
a Venetian ceiling by Tiepolo.

The grey – scrolled now
with silver-gilt – parts on
a blue so ethereal, so
tranquil, it can hardly be
credited, framed in stronger rose.

Then flocks of white proceed,
slowly mending the pearl, the grey
as the pink, hotter now, and
the blue, less fragile, dissolve
in lowering canopies of black.

## The Young Lovers on Whit Sunday

Next morning, the young lovers,
pleased with themselves, rise
late, wander with arms around
each other's waists, and lightly kiss
in the streets of the Old Town.
Or with indissolubly linked hands
– elephants ambling trunk to tail –
stop at every window in the Mall
then go on strolling aimlessly,
making all part before them.

How long will it last,
this paltry joy that seems to them
so earth-shaking?
– I give them three weeks.

## In Memory of Yamaguchi Takeyoshi
*Librarian*

For you, all life
was a library without walls,
each book a window on humanity,
each periodical an open door
upon an ever-larger world
in which you worked together with
your fellow men, a union of other
guardians of the word, and those
who had been stricken from the start
with handicaps far greater than
my own deep incapacity
to live within societies in which
I feel myself a total stranger.

So I shall remember you
always, for you simply accepted me,
as you did them, without commiseration,
but with pure concern
and practical affection,
giving of yourself generously,
so unfailingly, without consideration
for your own advantage,
till there was nothing left to give,
and in your delicate body
the great heart was still.

So we shall remember you,
in time's great library without walls.

## Across the Border

Those clouds have started coming over again
in sinister shapes – dinosaurs, death-ships,
or like lumps of brown rock, pear-shaped,
just hanging there, slow and heavy, gradually changing
into herds of monsters with red sunset veins. More and more
come long and swift, of a ghostly whiteness, forked beards,
frizzled hanks of hair from bleeding scalps.

They are coming with messages, mirages
of distant disturbances and meteor impacts,
unnatural calamities across the border
where the peaks curtain the east with ice –
that region like a running sore, where we fear
the worst, where everything can happen, and wars
rage on without our knowing why, or caring.

The messages were clear enough to be ignored, for
they were only clouds, the marvellous clouds.
We know what they are trying to tell us
but we shall not act upon their sunset warnings.
– They who are suffering are out of sight
and usually out of mind – their clouds are not ours,
whose intrusions on our peace can not be tolerated.

## Divided Sonnet

Here poets hauntingly identify
their startling nudity with other ghosts,
level the rich interior of eyes
there thinkingly where columns could be phrased
with statuary on the slotted coasts,
moonlike deracinate the relaxed sea
and charm the rooted wave because they must.

They all have lovely names, but none may seize
the voice you wanted me to know, who lend
a halting shower-music to the spoons
and turn whorled stairways into marble winds,
remembering the tragic sense of stone.
– Now sea-edge sucks to death the rigid corn
that hungered for the head beneath the sands.

## In the Planetarium

The voice of the absent commentator
is the voice of God at the console
as he manipulates levers and switches
that keep the stars in their courses.

The sky carries us with it
as the planets move in time
to a music of the spheres (Holst
of course) – and we move with them –

in and out of light and dark,
a sunny, leaf-dappled path through space
or a highroad of moonlit mica
or rail tracks to Möbius strip infinity.

## Ark

A sunset cloud becomes a shadowy tree,
suspends a leaning trunk on air, and spreads
its branches, twigs and fans of leaves across
the double screen of the entire sky
commanding a sense of balance in composition
worthy of some great oriental master
who almost imperceptibly lets it change
and dissolve into a shapeless
maze converting time and space into
estuaries with innumerable mouths
greeting the ark of the new moon.

# Flute Playing on a Moonlit Lake

The air is water
the waves are sky

a boat hangs
in emptiness

sound of a flute
rippling

a servant's
silken paddle

high above a full moon
reflected in the lake below

the dreaming boat –
is he playing his flute

to the moon or
to its reflection?

(Painting attributed to Zhao Danian, Ming dynasty, 14th-15th century.
Album leaf in ink and slight colour on silk. British Museum.
Reproduced in *The Brush Dances and the Ink Sings*.)

## In An Art Dealer's Window

Auden's ravaged face –
an action-painting savaged
by Jackson Pollock

late period tracks
of bicycle tyres and worn
rubbersoled sneakers

gritty and grubby
limestone lithograph of years –
mortuary bust

whose massive headpiece
has weathered into a grim
featureless grotesque

dripping with dark rains –
a blank ruin except for
the lost eyes looking.

## A Last Wish

I often wanted to
cut somebody's head off
so as to hear the sound
of blood streaming
from the jugular with
the whistle of wind
through wintry pines.

I never expected
I should finally hear it
rushing and screaming from
my own neck.

## Two Kinds of Suffering

The humility of objects
shames me into silence,
into self-effacement.
Like this cup with the broken handle,
still usable, but wounded in its integrity.

I sip from its cracked lip,
the cup without a loop
and it burns my fingers
scalds my mouth – yet I go on holding it
and even add more boiling water.

My favourite cup.
It is just an ordinary object, scarred
by life, and this is the one way we communicate,
through the numb exercise of pain –
two kinds of suffering.

## Accordionist

He lays his unshaven cheek
against the breathing lungs
on his animal, his pet that purrs
and murmurs as he amorously
kneads it with sudden passion –
throwing back his head and smiling
fleetingly at the beast's responses.

Then crouching close to the pearly stops
he listens to the creature's panting heart
as if trying to measure all the sadness in
the absent words of a faded chanson – and in
a shadow of the forgotten maker's breath.

## Submarine Time Capsule

Doomed deeper than a diving-bell
sounding the depths of the lost Marianas,
a marine time-capsule's rusted shell
rests in the stillness of seaweed lianas.

Nothing disturbs its profound meditation
in densest dark where no current reaches.
No one remembers its lonely location
far from the glitter of holiday beaches.

Yet there it lies like a submarine shipment
of pressurized helmets all drifted with sands.
Its dynamo's dead and its useless equipment
held in the fingers of skeleton hands.

Chock-full of rubbish from nineteen-twenty,
a junk-shop collection of clockwork mice,
a fleamarket banquet of bottles, all empty,
a crystal-set wireless and buckets for ice.

What was its purpose? What message are sharing
the overturned teacups, the beds all undone?
– And why is that gramophone trumpet still blaring
"Yo-ho-ho and a bottle of rum"?

## Wakened by a Poem

Somewhere in the middle of nowhere night
and when I was far from what is never home
I was awakened by the recurring nightmare
of a new poem, one that had been growing
unknown to me, like some grave indisposition
waiting to announce its fevers and infections.

In the darkness I started to compose
its title, crossed out, its first line,
its second line, redrafted, then another,
until I realized it would not wait till dawn,
had to be attended to there and then.

As I lay in my alien bed, I could recall
a pen and notebook on the reception desk
and they seemed to draw me onwards in the dark
(I couldn't find the foreign switches)
like a sleepwalker, hands outstretched
to feel my way and to receive what I imagined
might be the comforting realities of ink and paper
amid the dream world's halogenic sharpness,
the anguish of impossible loves, bleak sorrows.

The poem was slowly overflowing
even as I rose from the futon, and took
uncertain, staggering steps towards the bathroom
where even more urgent matters required
only a distracted attention in the darkness
as the poem began rushing through my mind
threatening to spill and be spent
before I could get its brute demands
at last on paper, in the first
flush of impulse.
                        Then my naked feet

traced a path on the wooden veranda floor
towards the night porter's desk, where the light
came on as soon as I entered the empty hall,
and I saw the pen, the visitors book
with one of my invented identities inscribed in it
and I started writing, page upon page,
relieved at last, and without touching the switch.

## Four Tanka by Sengai

To draw bamboo, one
rule exists. What is that rule?
The Buddha has said:
"To draw without a rule is
the one fundamental rule."

When an east wind blows,
the scent of plum blossom wafts
as far as China.
– The guardian of plum blossoms
carries a spray in his sleeve.

Han-shan and Shi-te:
sweeping does not clear the dust.
Reading sacred texts
does not allow the reader
to learn how to read letters.

To grasp their meaning
just by reading the sacred
texts – impossible?
– Sweeping dust away with brooms
alone is impossible.

## Death of the Artist

At the bottom of her unkempt garden
the studio still faces north.
No blinds at the windows. Only
shifting shadows of lilacs draw their shades.

It remains just as she left it.
She had no family, no friends,
not even a dog, a cat, a plant to care for.
She was the painter of lonelinesses, absences.

The doors, still wide open, welcoming
like all the doors and windows in her life
that rarely welcomed anyone. "Nothing worth taking."
– Only a few unfinished failures.

But in the winter twilight, a procession
of freshly-primed canvases, their white
dusted, as she liked them to be
before she started the first blind moves.

They stand like the wings of a theatre –
virgin, haunted, untouchable now.
These were the guardians of the memories,
the lost dreams she painted out of the dark

of solitude, the screens of secret griefs and joys
that only she could tell.
                    Now she has gone,
leaving the doors wide open to fog and rain,
no one else can frame the emptiness she leaves.

## In Memory of Lindley Williams Hubbell

Not a single window lighted
in the mountain villages, whose lanes
are dark as furrows in the barren fields. But moonlight
silvers panes of broken glass, and roofs
tiled with native slate: and somewhere
a bonfire smoulders in parched ravines,
a tree glows with pale blossom in old snow.
And in ancient half-ruined churches
a candle burns, a crucifix glitters
in reflected radiance from a leaded lancet.

The sleeping faith is somehow kept alive
amid indifference, neglect and scorn
while the silent bells hang sullenly
like heavy fruit in their open gables
of a land too poor for steeples.
                              But even here
someone now awakens before dawn, begins to kindle fire
in a hearth never completely cold.

## The Automobile Graveyard in the Snow

They look finally at rest, after their last
sidetrip – the abandoned Fords, Renaults, Toyotas
whose faded reds and battered blues
baked and blistered in summer afternoons.

Their grubby creams and rusted ivory whites,
their shattered windscreens and rearview mirrors
that had an evil glitter in the city moonlight
bear now a new paint job of pristine purity
covering the cracks and dents and crumpled fenders:
at peace at last in the overhauling blizzard.

They lie there, peaceful, their own memorials.
The nesting birds fly in and out of
what was once a lovers' hideaway,
and on the tumbled rooftops
pattern their cryptic elegies.

## Beijing Flu

I lie night after night
listening for the next spasm –
how musical the strings of phlegm,
the keyboards of cataarh!

I have been bringing up gobbets
of the stuff, in variegated shades –
mid-brown, quivering like sand-froth,
an almost violet tone, then
rancid green, quite fashionable,
sulfurous yellow turning
to apricot or over-ripe persimmon,
olive streaked with red –
all the colours of some hellish prism.

On my microscope
they look like nothing on earh
(which is what they are).

But it is the sounds they make –
most appealing yet appalling.
Sometimes in my fever I think
it's the couple downstairs arguing,
or children shouting on a distant street
or an idiotic cartoon jingle –
or is it birds? Or dogs barking in the mist?
Or voices from the past, the Forbidden City?

I can't sleep for listening
to the next voice, incorporate,
perhaps coming from Arcturus.

## Reading Old Poems

Reading again the poems I wrote
when I was young and full of invention –
it is the first time I have looked at them
since they were published nearly fifty years ago.

They bring back all the youthful force
and hope, yearning, tenderness
of that vanished era, their purity
touching me now to tears.

There is nothing I would change.
All seem to me perfect – only
my subjects have changed,
changed as I have, changed as life.

It is like looking at old
sepia photographs of childhood –
so much innocence, fresh beauty.
Yet within my heart and soul

I know there is still that core of truth
undefiled, inexhaustible well of love
for life and all its manifestations,
a deep spring of poetry ever flowing.

Perhaps, though I cannot compare
with Yeats, Valéry, Rilke – all who stopped
then started over again, as I have always done –
my poetry is beginning to take another turn.

These old poems move me to tears
of pride in my art, of gratitude, regret
that they are not better known –
sadness that they are all now out of print.

## The Prompter

On stage, but not of it
she camps on her little stool
in the stifling hooded box
and knows entire repertoires –
plays, operas, one-man shows
better than any performer.

She acts the parts with them.
She knows all the cues, the beats
between the lines, all the business,
the moves, the lighting, the exits
and entrances. She notes the fluffs
but can do nothing about that.

She feels instinctively when
an actor will forget his lines,
sees at his first entrance
that he is not altogether
in possession of his part, or of himself –
worries about love, money, family, fickle fame.

She could take over any role,
male or female, stand-in for star
or utility. She has a certain timbre,
a pitch of voice that carries just enough
to be heard on stage, not off. But if she wishes
she could recite the entire drama

to the patient audience, play all night
to the gallery, and take a bow – a dream
she never realizes, up there in her little box.

**The Death of Max Jacob**
*(Quimper 1876 – Drancy 1944)*

He called himself "the Celtic Jew".
In his last photograph, we see him
like Chaplin, in a baggy dark suit,
clumsy boots, shirt, tie, carrying a homburg.
Stitched on his broad left lapel a yellow diamond
bearing the word "Jew".

Converted to Roman Catholicism – religion
that allowed him to sin daily and be redeemed –
his life was one long lapse into painting
and recovery in poetry, his true faith,
one he never changed. "Sincerity," he said,
"means having your subject in your very blood."

Thursday 24 Februay 1944. The Gestapo
descended upon Mme Persillard's house, where
he had been a lodger since 1939. Benoît-sur-Loire.
Refusing to make an escape through the back garden, Max
preferred to have the police discover him
seated writing poetry at his work table.

Told to pack a suitcase. A friend gives him
a flask of spirits and his own warm underpants.
His landlady – "Now look what's happened!
Fat lot of good all your praying did you!" –
ran to warn the curé and his vicar: "At least one of them
might have come, it was only a cheap funeral they were doing."

She made her lodger take one of her best blankets.
"The main thing," says Max as he departs, "is that I made
a good impression upon my landlady Mme Persillard."
– Military prison, Orléans, concentration camp, Drancy.

Cocteau, Guitry, Jouhandeau petition for his release.
His old friend Picasso says: "It's no use doing anything."

6 March the Gestapo signs an order for his release.
"Max is an angel," Picasso had said. "He has no need of us
to escape from prison." – His deportation to Auschwitz
had been set for 7 March. But he had died in the camp infirmary,
at Drancy, of pneumonia, the day before the order for release.
Orders of release are always meant to arrive too late.

## Birthdays

As you grow older, looking ever
younger for your age, on birthdays
you begin to get more candles than cake;
more book tokens, less liqueur bonbons.
Instead, an ever-increasing avalanche
of those greeting cards graded by numbers
in the upper tens – full tally of years
cruelly emblazoned upon them in tasteful
dignified abstract compositions, paper urns.

"On your 87th birthday," they inform me,
"all at the Laburnums wish you many of them..."
Many of what? It's getting past a joke.
– And in the blazing forest of candles
stuck in a greenish moss of synthetic cream
there is a sinister flickering.
– I haven't the wind to blow them all out
at a single breath. They seem to take
a whole lifetime to extinguish.

## The Sleep of Reason

Sometimes dreaming I am drafting poems –
the way my father the joiner would dream
he was planing planks, or chiselling joints
for the new army barracks window frames –

finding myself absently beginning
to feel my way through the entangling sheets
of blank paper to some kind of margin –
threshold to be overstepped with caution

of first words' unexpected bravado.
– Itching fingers scratch invisible lines
that may or may not rhyme without reason
propose no beginning yet obscurely

linked to hidden messages mutely masked
by mystic madrigals that tick the tune
of one lost foot one syllable of sweat –
that blink of vision mistrusting its own

dark meanings in the long tunnels of slumber
flashing permanently diminishing
living daylights lost in endless endings
with moth lanterns signalling endless darks

in the sleep of reason that awakens
memories beyond craft, beyond draftings
of lost deliriums, phantasmal dawns –
waking clueless in sinister half-light

deafened speechless by the sudden silence
of my absent father planing his planks
and chiselling joints with his joiner's touch
leaving this lost scent of freshly-planed wood.

## Poet Acrobat

To the brassy orchestras of his daily life
He goes through the usual paces high above
non-existent audiences holding their breath
while he keeps wasting his upon the dead paper
white with fright formed by all those upturned masks waiting
for the next death-defying dive – in a silence
deep as a grave's, as he balances his books of
still unwritten words on time's treacherous trapeze

in unspeakable messages of warning, or
wonder, or simply personal worries that he
tries effortlessly to keep to himself – the one
self he has – while the silent human audiences
always hesitating to applaud those efforts
he appears to make so effortless, still sit
gaping at hands outstretched to the Big Top's only
heaven – his one support in life's shrill silences.

## Final Curtain

Now when I wake up
I do so against my will –
autodestruction
without all the bother of
having to do it myself

is my ideal –
a farewell that is neither
frivolous nor fond
but a simple decision
never to wake up from sleep

that is already
more than indulgent slumber
but deliberate
self-sacrificing absence
from ever-present mess

of mind and motive –
no theatricality
but the simple drop
of breath's curtain on a stage
already dark and empty.

## A Graveyard in the Floods
*(tanka)*

In dense mists of dawn
there is a phantasmal gloom
        over the graveyard –
supernatural radiance
reflected from the waters

        on the old graveyard
now drowning under the floods
        from rivers roaring
at this crossing where they meet
and start to fight each other

        to find free passage
through this forest of mossed stones –
        gravestones all standing
up to the sculptured angels
decorating drowning dates

        in raging torrents
that obliterate the names,
        dates, verses, mossed lists
of the departed ones' lost
career records – wife, children –

        names now utterly
dilapidated, not by
        time or weather, but
by this fury of floods that
shake the very foundations

        of all these marbled
monuments grown stained
        with time – lost birth dates

obliterated death dates
ancestral records all mossed

    sinking out of sight
beneath this ever-rising
        indifferent tide
of forgotten memories
and names, once bright, now vanished.

## Final Scores

A life spent battling with
cheap plastic shower curtains
in strange hotels for transients.

If that were the only thing
I had to battle against
there would be little cause to complain.

"Not much catch, is it?"
My father's grim comment on
life and loss come back to me

with his bitter smile – the smile
I strive not to imitate, as I try
to keep quiet the sarcastic bark

which was what he used for laughter,
while my mother favoured wordless
mirth not too far from tears.

\*\*\*

Now they were the ones who really
had something worth complaining about –
a son who grew strange to them

and to himself, although he was just
following his inner voices –
voices foreign to them and to their world.

"I don't know where he gets it from..."
as I overheard my father complaining.
"Not from our side of the family..."

was my mother's retort.
– What were they talking about?
I realized it must be me

and I moved silently away from the door
so that I would hear no more. I took
my overdue books back to the library.

\*\*\*

For their just concern was
nothing to do with me. I knew
I could only be myself, and no one else –

certainly not the personage
they apparently had in mind for me
as an infinitely suitable son for them.

And after all, what right had they
to make me what they wanted their own
narrow respectable world to admire?

"A safe job for life at the Town Hall"
was their ideal for their only child
who obviously was becoming in need of

some kind of protection from himself and
what they perceived as the wicked world
beyond the cosy Tyneside ghetto

from which I knew I must escape
"some sunny day", before it was too late
for me, not soon enough for them.

\*\*\*

After his death, I read my father's
pocket diaries, his laboured penmanship.
He mentions everybody in our family

but only my name is never there
among the visits to the dole queue,
the dawn journeys to distant jobs

that only lasted a week or two,
the meetings at his 'club' with the 'brethren'
of the Amalgamated Society of Woodworkers.

But I did not exist in his little world
of the Pools, which he never won,
whose losses he scrupulously recorded.

(The only thing I was good for was
to fill in his Pool coupons. Superstitiously,
he believed my ignorance would bring him luck.)

\*\*\*

But it never did. My own reward
was to have to listen to
the Saturday night litany

of wins, draws, losses, matches
cancelled, over our old wireless set
while he sat marking the fixtures lists

in *The South Shields Gazette and Shipping
Telegraph* with his carpenter's
flat chisel-point indelible pencil.

Those radio recitations were like a dirge
to me. And still, when I happen to hear
its dismal monologue of weekly defeat

it fills my heart with rage and sorrow
for a father I never really knew,
whose bond with his only son was dead loss...

\*\*\*

Sheffield Wednesday three, Carlisle one,
Aston Villa two, Arsenal two, Heart of
Midlothian nil, Liverpool nil, Newcastle nil...